readers

Who's in Your Class?

By Susan Blackaby

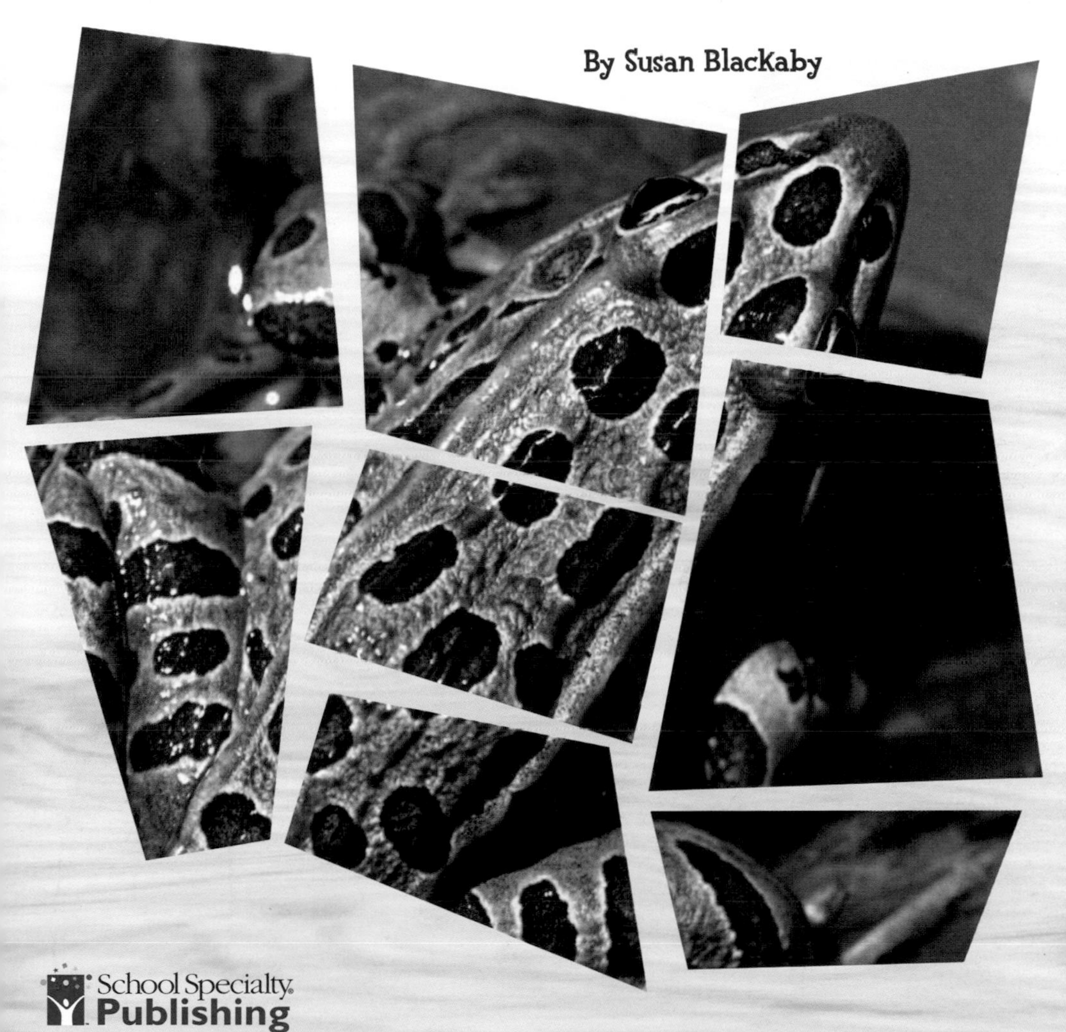

School Specialty Publishing

Library of Congress Cataloging-in-Publication Data is on file with the publisher.

Send all inquiries to:
School Specialty Publishing
8720 Orion Place
Columbus, OH 43240-2111

ISBN 0-7696-4244-6

1 2 3 4 5 6 7 8 9 10 PHXBK 12 11 10 09 08 07 06

Hi, I'm a manatee.
Join me in learning about
the different animal families in nature.
Can you guess how I am like a mouse,
a bear, or an elephant?
Well, we all belong to the mammal family, just like you!
Turn the page to learn more about
the animal families in nature.

Table of Contents

Vertebrates

Mammals 4–11
Birds 12–17
Amphibians 18–21
Reptiles 22–25
Fish 26–27

Invertebrates

Invertebrates 28–29

Thinking About It 31–32

Vertebrates

There are two main types of animals—
animals with backbones and animals
without backbones.
Animals with backbones are **vertebrates**.
One of the biggest groups of vertebrates
is **mammals**.
All mammals are alike in three important ways.
They are warm-blooded.
They have hair or fur.
The mothers produce milk to feed their young.
Although a coyote and a chimpanzee may seem
very different, they are both mammals.

Manatee Mentions

Chimpanzees are **primates**. Primates are a kind of mammal. Other primates include apes, monkeys, and human beings.

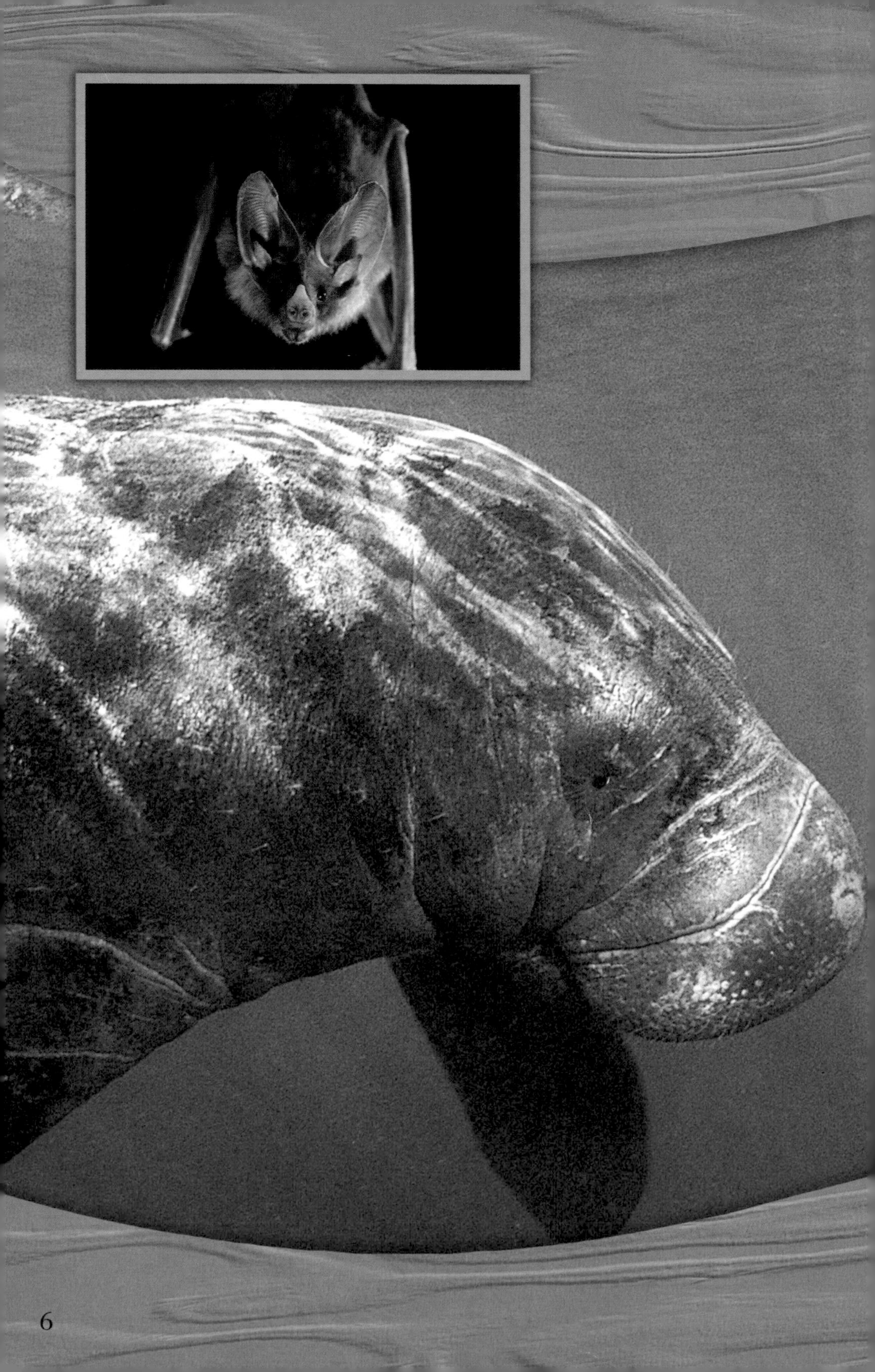

Mammals

There are many different kinds of mammals.
Some mammals, such as manatees,
spend their lives in the water.
These mammals are **cetaceans** (sih-TAY-shuhns).
Cetaceans have flippers and a tail with flukes
for swimming and diving in the water.
Cetaceans live in the water,
but like other mammals,
they have lungs and breathe air.

Manatee Mentions

There are about 4,000 **species** of mammals. Bats are mammals, too. They are the only mammal that can fly.

Some mammals are **marsupials**.
Marsupials are different from other mammals in a special way.
They have pocket-like pouches.
A baby marsupial is very tiny when it is born.
It climbs into its mother's pouch.
It stays inside her pouch while it grows bigger and stronger.
Kangaroos and koalas are marsupials.
So are wombats and Tasmanian devils.

Manatee Mentions

Most marsupials live in Australia and South America. The Virginia opossum is the only native-born marsupial found in North America.

Most adult mammals give birth to babies.
Cats give birth to kittens.
Bears give birth to cubs.
Dolphins give birth to calves.
But some mammals are different.
These mammals lay eggs.
Then, the eggs hatch into baby mammals.
Egg-laying mammals belong to a small group of animals called **monotremes**.

Manatee Mentions

The spiny anteater and the duck-billed platypus are the only mammals in the monotreme family.

Birds

Birds are another group of vertebrates.
Birds are warm-blooded animals that lay eggs.
Birds are the only animals with feathers.
Feathers keep birds warm.
They also help most birds to fly.
Some birds live on or near the water.
These birds are called *waterbirds*.
Waterbirds, such as snow geese, are good swimmers.
So are ducks and swans.
Some waterbirds, such as herons, have long legs.
Long legs help them wade in shallow water.

Manatee Mentions

Waterbirds naturally produce a special oil. This oil makes their feathers waterproof.

Waterbirds catch and eat fish.
Some birds eat fruits and seeds.
Other birds, called **raptors**, eat small animals, such as mice and other birds.
These birds are also known as "birds of prey."
Raptors include hawks, eagles, owls, vultures, and osprey.
These birds hunt well.
They have good eyesight.
They have powerful wings.
Their feet have claws to grab their prey.
Their beaks are hooked to tear their food.

Manatee Mentions

Most owls hunt at night. But the snowy owl, shown above, hunts during the day. The snowy owl's white feathers help it blend into the snow.

Bluebirds and hummingbirds are perching birds.
Perching birds make up the largest group of birds.
These birds are named for the shape of their feet.
They have four toes on each foot.
Three toes point forward.
One toe points backward.
Perching birds use their toes to grab
and hold onto things.
This keeps them from falling off tree branches
and telephone wires.

Manatee Mentions

A hummingbird beats its wings 60-70 times per second. Its wings beat so fast that they make a humming sound!

Amphibians

Amphibians are cold-blooded vertebrates.
They live on land and in water.
When in the water, amphibians breathe
through gills.
When on land, they use lungs to breathe.
Frogs and toads make up a large group
of amphibians.
They live along the edges of streams and ponds.
Frogs have wet, smooth skin.
They have strong back legs for hopping.
Toads have dry, bumpy skin.
They have short back legs and don't hop
as much as frogs.

Manatee Mentions

Amphibians have been around for a long time. Fossils show that amphibians probably lived on the earth 375 million years ago!

Salamanders are another group of amphibians.
Salamanders have long bodies and long tails.
They have short legs.
Their skin feels wet and smooth.
Some salamanders spend all of their lives
in the water.
Others live both on land and in the water.
Caecilians (seh-SILL-yens) are also a kind
of amphibian.
They look like large earthworms, but they have
jaws and teeth.

Manatee Mentions

Some salamanders grow to be five feet long, as tall as a person!

Reptiles

Reptiles are another group of vertebrates.
Reptiles are cold-blooded.
They lie in warm places where they can get lots of sun.
Reptiles have dry, scaly skin.
They lay eggs that have thick shells.
When a baby reptile is born, it looks like a small version of an adult reptile.
Alligators, crocodiles, turtles, tortoises, snakes, and lizards are all reptiles.

Manatee Mentions

The American alligator is the biggest reptile in the United States. It can reach up to 18 feet in length, longer than 5 children lying down head to foot.

Lizards make up the biggest group of reptiles.
Lizards come in all sizes, colors, and shapes.
They look like salamanders but have dry, scaly skin.
Lizards have claws, ear openings, and eyelids.
Lizards and snakes are closely related.
Snakes have long, scaly bodies.
They do not have legs, and they do not have ear openings.
About 115 species of snakes live in the United States.
Only 17 species are poisonous.

Manatee Mentions

The snake shown in the photograph is a copperhead. Its bite is poisonous. A copperhead's bite can cause pain and illness, but it seldom kills a person.

Fish

Fish are vertebrates that spend their lives in water.
They are able to breathe underwater through gills.
Gills soak up oxygen from the water.
Almost all fish have fins.
Fins help fish to swim through the water.
Fish are divided into two groups—
fish with jaws and fish without jaws.
Lampreys and hagfish are jawless fish.
All other fish are jawed fish.
Some jawed fish, such as the shark, have skeletons
made of **cartilage**, or tough, stretchy tissue.
Others, such as the sea horse, have bony skeletons.

Manatee Mentions

There are more than 21,000 species of fish. There are more kinds of fish than all of the other kinds of vertebrates put together.

Invertebrates

Invertebrates are animals
that do not have backbones.
Jellyfish, worms, and centipedes are invertebrates.
So are caterpillars and butterflies.
Most invertebrates are **arthropods**.
Their bodies are divided into sections.
Thin, hard shells protect their soft body parts.
All insects are arthropods.
So are shellfish, such as the shrimp shown above.

Manatee Mentions

Most of the animals on the earth are invertebrates.
There are more than one million known species
of invertebrates.

Vocabulary

amphibian–a cold-blooded animal that spends its life in water and on land. *A frog is an amphibian.*

arthropod–an animal without a backbone that has a segmented body and a hard outer shell. *A spider is an arthropod.*

cartilage–a tough, stretchy tissue that forms part of the skeleton of animals and people. *A shark's skeleton is made entirely of cartilage.*

cetacean–a mammal that lives in water. *A whale is a cetacean.*

invertebrate–an animal without a backbone. *An insect is an invertebrate.*

mammal–an animal with an internal skeleton and backbone that breathes air through lungs, and feeds its young on milk. *A human being is a mammal.*

marsupial–a mammal of the order *Marsupialia*. Females have pouches outside their bellies to carry their young after birth. *A kangaroo is a marsupial.*

monotreme–a mammal that lays eggs. *A spiny anteater is a monotreme.*

primate–a mammal of the order *Primates*, including monkeys, apes, and human beings, that has a large brain and flexible hands. *A monkey is a primate.*

raptor–a bird of prey that hunts and kills other animals. *The large raptor swooped down to catch the mouse.*

reptile–an animal with scaly skin and an internal skeleton arranged around a backbone. It breathes air through its lungs. *A snake is a reptile.*

species–a group of living things that have similar traits. *A human being is a species of mammal.*

vertebrate–an animal that has a backbone. *A cat is a vertebrate.*

Think About It!

1. What three things do mammals have in common?
2. How are cetaceans different from fish? How are they similar?
3. How are birds different from bats? How are they similar?
4. Name three animals that are amphibians. Name three animals that are reptiles.
5. Which family do insects belong to?

The Story and You!

1. What characteristics make you a mammal?
2. What is your favorite vertebrate animal? What is your favorite invertebrate animal? Why?
3. If you were to hold an animal fair, which animals from the book would you include? Why?
4. How is an animal family similar to your own family?